Mark Margolis

A biography

Scribe paradise

Table of contents

Brief history of mark Margolis

Mark Margolis, born in Philadelphia in 1939 to Russian and Polish Jewish immigrants, had an early passion for acting. He honed his skills in school plays and local theatre productions before taking a leap of faith and moving to New York City to pursue a career in acting after high school.

In New York, Margolis attended the prestigious Actors Studio and learned from renowned acting teachers like Stella Adler and Lee Strasberg. His dedication and talent paid off, and in 1966, he made his Broadway debut. Margolis's career continued to flourish with numerous appearances in other Broadway productions.

As the 1970s rolled around, Margolis transitioned into film and television work. He delivered memorable performances in films like "Scarface," "Pi," and "Requiem for a Dream." On the small screen, he graced television shows such as "Oz," "The Sopranos," and eventually landed his most iconic role as Hector Salamanca in "Breaking Bad" and "Better Call Saul."

Hector Salamanca, the wheelchair-bound drug lord who communicated by ringing a bell, became Mark Margolis's most famous character. His portrayal received critical acclaim and earned him an Emmy nomination in 2012. Throughout the years, Margolis has consistently showcased his versatility as an actor, taking on diverse roles and portraying complex characters with intensity and depth.

Even as the years passed, Margolis didn't slow down. He continued to work in both film and television, delivering stellar performances in projects like "Noah" and "The Irishman." He kept viewers captivated with appearances in shows like "American Horror Story: Asylum" and "Your Honor."

Mark Margolis's journey in the entertainment industry is a testament to hard work, dedication, and the power of talent. He has left a lasting impact on the world of acting and remains a respected figure in the industry. His story is indeed inspiring, proving that with passion and perseverance, one can achieve greatness and leave a lasting legacy in the hearts of audiences and fellow actors alike.

Introduction

Mark Margolis was a multi-talented artist, renowned for his acting, directing, and writing skills. His true gift was his ability to breathe life into stories, effortlessly immersing audiences in the emotions of the characters he portrayed. Through his performances, he could evoke laughter, tears, and even fear.

Among his most famous roles was Hector Salamanca in "Breaking Bad," a character who became iconic in the AMC series. As a wheelchair-bound drug lord, Hector communicated through a bell, and Margolis's portrayal was nothing short of exceptional. He infused the role with a sense of menace and power, leaving a lasting impact on viewers.

One unforgettable moment was in the "Better Call Saul" episode when Hector, sitting in a nursing home, sees a commercial for a wheelchair lift. In a display of pettiness, he rings his bell, summoning a nurse to bring him the TV remote. When the nurse refuses, Hector rings the bell again, resulting in a heart attack. The scene was simultaneously humorous and disturbing, showcasing Hector's cunning and control despite his physical limitations.

Margolis's performance as Hector inspired countless memes and GIFs, demonstrating the enduring impact of his work on fans of the show. His versatility as an actor allowed him to embody various characters convincingly, leaving indelible marks in each role he played.

Aside from acting, Margolis also shone as a director and writer. His passing was a significant loss to the entertainment industry, as he brought joy and entertainment to millions. Nevertheless, his stories and performances will continue to resonate with audiences for generations to come.

In addition to his portrayal of Hector Salamanca, other audience-favourite moments from Margolis's career included his roles as Alberto "The Shadow" in "Scarface" (1983), Antonio Nappa in "Oz" (1997-2003), Mr. Kaplan in "The Sopranos" (1999-2007), Mr. Gold in "American Horror Story: Asylum" (2012-2013), and Angelo Cardinale in "The Irishman" (2019). Each character showcased Margolis's remarkable talent and made an impact on viewers.

Mark Margolis's legacy is not just that of a skilled actor, but also of a master storyteller who touched the hearts and minds of audiences worldwide. His work will remain a source of joy and inspiration for years to come, ensuring that his memory lives on through his stories and the emotions he elicited in those who experienced his art.

Chapter 1: Early Life

Mark Margolis's early life in Philadelphia was marked by cultural diversity, a supportive family, and a strong passion for the arts. Born on November 26, 1939, to Russian and Polish Jewish immigrants, Margolis grew up in a tight-knit, working-class neighbourhood. He shared his upbringing with a sister, and his parents, recognizing his interest in acting, fostered his dreams from an early age.

In the Philadelphia of his youth, Margolis attended public schools and quickly found his calling in the world of performance. From school plays to local theatre productions, he showcased his talent and captivated audiences with his early performances. As the young actor honed his skills, his parents saw the potential in his talent and supported his ambitions, even helping him finance acting classes to nurture his gift.

Margolis's exposure to the diverse cultures and experiences of Philadelphia's melting pot contributed significantly to his development as an actor. Interacting with people from various backgrounds instilled in him a profound sense of empathy and understanding, qualities that later shone through in his performances, allowing him to immerse himself deeply into the characters he portrayed.

With a strong connection to the arts, Margolis attended the Philadelphia High School for the Creative and Performing Arts. This specialised institution allowed him to explore and refine his skills in theatre and dance, further solidifying his passion for performance. His active involvement in the city's theatre scene during his formative years provided him with invaluable experiences and a profound love for the stage.

In 1966, Margolis took his first step into the illustrious world of Broadway, making his debut in "The Effect of Gamma Rays on Man-in-the-Moon Marigolds." This marked the beginning of a successful Broadway career that included notable productions such as "The Crucible," "A Chorus Line," and "Torch Song Trilogy."

As the 1970s arrived, Margolis broadened his horizons, venturing into film and television. His remarkable talent landed him roles in notable films like "Scarface," "Pi," and "Requiem for a Dream," where he left a lasting impression on the silver screen. His versatility and acting prowess also garnered him opportunities in popular television series such as "Oz," "The Sopranos," and the critically acclaimed "Breaking Bad," where he delivered a tour de force performance as Hector Salamanca.

The character of Hector Salamanca became one of Mark Margolis's most celebrated roles. The wheelchair-bound drug lord who communicated through the ring of a bell showcased Margolis's ability to embody complex characters with intensity and depth. The depth of his portrayal earned him an Emmy nomination for Outstanding Guest Actor in a Drama Series in 2012.

In recent years, Margolis continued to be active in the entertainment industry, with notable roles in films like "Noah" and "The Irishman," as well as appearances in television shows like "American Horror Story: Asylum" and "Your Honor."

Throughout his career, Mark Margolis remained a versatile and respected actor, consistently demonstrating his commitment to his craft. His performances were characterised by an emotional intensity that left audiences captivated and moved. His life journey from Philadelphia to Broadway, from the silver screen to television, showcased his resilience and dedication to his art.

Indeed, Margolis's childhood in Philadelphia laid the foundation for a successful and impactful career. The city's cultural richness, along with the unwavering support of his family, played a crucial role in shaping him into the talented storyteller that the world came to know and admire. As the curtain rose on his life's stage, Mark Margolis continued to captivate and inspire, leaving a lasting legacy that would resonate for generations to come.

His Parents

Mark Margolis's parents, Isidore Margolis and Fanya Fried, played pivotal roles in shaping the man he became. Isidore Margolis was born in Russia in 1907 and immigrated to the United States in 1913. He settled in Philadelphia, where he worked as a skilled tailor, providing for his family with hard work and dedication. His experiences as an immigrant navigating a new country instilled in him resilience and an unwavering commitment to providing a better life for his loved ones.

Fanya Fried, born in Poland in 1910, also immigrated to the United States, arriving in 1920. She became a homemaker, dedicating herself to nurturing her children and creating a warm and loving home for the family. Fanya's nurturing nature and dedication to her family undoubtedly influenced Mark, leaving a lasting impact on his compassionate and empathetic approach to life and acting.

His Sister

Mark Margolis's sister, Elaine Margolis, born in 1941, was his confidante and steadfast supporter throughout his life. The bond between Mark and Elaine was exceptionally close, and their relationship served as a source of emotional strength for both of them. Elaine pursued a career as a teacher and, like her parents, instilled a love of learning and knowledge in her students. Her dedication to education and her passion for teaching likely played a role in shaping Mark's appreciation for storytelling and communication through acting.

Parents and Siblings' Influence on His Life and Career

Growing up in a family of immigrants, Mark Margolis witnessed firsthand the challenges and triumphs of building a life in a new country. His parents' journey instilled in him a deep understanding and empathy for the immigrant experience, which he would later channel into his portrayals of characters from diverse backgrounds.

Isidore Margolis's work ethic and determination to provide for his family served as a role model for Mark, inspiring him to pursue his dreams with dedication and perseverance. Fanya Fried's nurturing presence and support allowed Mark to explore his artistic interests and thrive as he developed his acting talent.

The close bond between Mark and Elaine was a source of unwavering encouragement for him. Elaine's own pursuit of a career in education likely influenced Mark's passion for storytelling and his desire to communicate meaningfully through his acting.

The support and guidance Mark received from his parents and sister were instrumental in his success as an actor. Their belief in him and their willingness to invest in his artistic education through acting classes helped pave the way for his impressive career on Broadway, in film, and on television.

In conclusion, Mark Margolis's parents and sister played pivotal roles in his life, providing a foundation of love, support, and cultural understanding that profoundly influenced his journey as an actor and storyteller. Their influence is evident in his deep empathy for his characters, his intense performances, and his ability to portray the human experience with authenticity. Mark's family provided him with the tools and inspiration to leave an indelible mark on the world of acting and entertainment.

His Early Interest in Acting

Mark Margolis's journey into the world of acting began at a young age, fueled by a natural inclination and nurtured by the support of his parents. As a child growing up in Philadelphia, he found himself captivated by the magic of the theatre and the transformative power of storytelling. This early interest blossomed into a passion that would guide him through a successful and impactful career as an actor.

One of the key influences on Margolis's early interest in acting was his parents' love for the theatre. As immigrants with a rich cultural background, they recognized the value of artistic expression and the importance of preserving and celebrating their heritage through the performing arts. Taking young Margolis to see plays became a cherished family tradition, igniting his imagination and igniting the spark of curiosity within him.

As Margolis stepped onto the stage for school plays and local theatre productions, it became evident that he possessed a natural talent for acting. He had an innate ability to inhabit characters fully, breathing life into them and making them believable to audiences. This skill set him apart and quickly garnered attention from the Philadelphia theatre scene, allowing him to ascend the ranks and gain valuable experience on the stage.

Beyond his innate talent, what truly set Mark Margolis apart was his ability to connect with audiences on an emotional level. His performances transcended the boundaries of the stage, touching the hearts and minds of those who witnessed his work. This emotional connection, combined with his acting prowess, left a lasting impact on viewers and solidified his place as a captivating performer.

The experiences of participating in school plays and local theatre productions were formative for Margolis. They allowed him to hone his craft, experiment with different roles, and learn from seasoned actors and directors. These early opportunities nurtured his passion for acting and laid the foundation for a successful career in the industry.

Mark Margolis's early interest in acting not only shaped his professional life but also became an enduring love that remained with him throughout his life. It provided him with a sense of purpose and fulfilment, inspiring him to continue honing his skills and delivering impactful performances that resonated with audiences worldwide.

In conclusion, Mark Margolis's early interest in acting was a harmonious blend of natural talent, parental support, and a deep appreciation for the transformative power of storytelling. It ignited a lifelong passion for the theatre, set him on a path to success, and allowed him to become a master storyteller, captivating and inspiring audiences with every role he took on. His journey from a young actor in Philadelphia to an acclaimed performer on the global stage is a testament to the enduring power of following one's passion and nurturing the early sparks of creativity.

Chapter 2: The Early Years

Mark Margolis's early years in Philadelphia were marked by cultural richness, family support, and a profound passion for the arts. Born on November 26, 1939, to Russian and Polish Jewish immigrants, Margolis's upbringing in a working-class neighbourhood exposed him to the diverse tapestry of life, a formative experience that would influence his acting and storytelling for years to come.

Growing up in Philadelphia, Margolis attended public schools, where he discovered his early interest in acting. It was within the realm of school plays and local theatre productions that his natural talent for the craft began to shine. His parents, Isidore and Fanya Margolis, were pivotal figures in nurturing his passion for the arts. As avid theatre lovers, they instilled in Mark an appreciation for storytelling and the power of the stage. Encouraged by his parents, Mark's interest in acting was supported and celebrated, setting the stage for his journey as a performer.

Isidore Margolis's profession as a tailor demanded hard work and perseverance, qualities that left a lasting impression on Mark. The example set by his father instilled a strong work ethic in him and fueled his determination to succeed as an actor. Fanya Margolis's role as a homemaker was equally crucial in fostering a warm and supportive environment, encouraging Mark to explore his artistic interests fearlessly.

As Mark's talent for acting continued to blossom, he swiftly ascended the ranks of the Philadelphia theatre scene, earning recognition and respect within the artistic community. He found solace and joy in performing, drawing on the cultural richness of his surroundings to bring depth and authenticity to his portrayals.

In 1966, Mark made his Broadway debut in "The Effect of Gamma Rays on Man-in-the-Moon Marigolds," an important milestone in his career. This marked the beginning of a successful journey on the grand stage, with notable appearances in other Broadway productions, including "The Crucible," "A Chorus Line," and "Torch Song Trilogy."

As the 1970s arrived, Margolis embarked on a new chapter, venturing into film and television. His performances in iconic films like "Scarface," "Pi," and "Requiem for a Dream" showcased his versatility as an actor. On the small screen, he captivated audiences with his roles in renowned television shows like "Oz," "The Sopranos," and the critically acclaimed "Breaking Bad," where his portrayal of Hector Salamanca became one of his most celebrated and unforgettable roles.

Margolis's intense and emotionally charged performances resonated with audiences, earning him critical acclaim and a devoted fan base. His ability to bring complex characters to life, including the enigmatic and wheelchair-bound Hector Salamanca, demonstrated the depth of his talent and the range of his abilities as a versatile actor.

Even in recent years, Mark Margolis continued to captivate audiences with his appearances in films like "Noah" and "The Irishman," and on television shows like "American Horror Story: Asylum" and "Your Honor."

His early years in Philadelphia, attending the Philadelphia High School for the Creative and Performing Arts and actively participating in the city's vibrant theatre scene, played a pivotal role in shaping his trajectory as an actor. The city's diverse cultures and experiences became the wellspring of empathy and understanding that he would infuse into his performances, allowing him to connect with audiences on a profound emotional level.

In conclusion, Mark Margolis's early years in Philadelphia laid the foundation for a remarkable and celebrated career in the entertainment industry. Supported by a loving family, he embraced his passion for acting, becoming a respected and versatile actor who left an indelible mark on Broadway, film, and television. His unwavering commitment to his craft and the love of performance instilled in him during his early years remained a constant driving force, ensuring that his legacy as a masterful storyteller will endure for generations to come.

Mark Margolis's Early Career in Theater

Mark Margolis's early career in theatre served as the bedrock of his journey as a seasoned actor. His passion for the arts and his natural talent propelled him to pursue formal training in theatre and dance at the Philadelphia High School for the Creative and Performing Arts. This decision marked the beginning of a transformative period in his life, igniting his love for performance and setting him on a path towards a remarkable career in the world of acting.

Embracing the vibrant theatre scene of Philadelphia, Margolis actively participated in a myriad of productions, honing his craft and captivating audiences with his performances. His dedication to his artistry quickly earned him recognition as one of the city's most gifted and promising actors.

His early years in theatre provided him with invaluable opportunities to collaborate with renowned actors and directors, exposing him to different acting styles and approaches. Working alongside such talented professionals enriched his understanding of the craft and allowed him to absorb valuable insights, which he would later bring to the stages of Broadway and beyond.

In 1966, Mark Margolis's talent and hard work paid off when he made his Broadway debut in "The Effect of Gamma Rays on Man-in-the-Moon Marigolds." This momentous milestone marked a significant step forward in his acting career and opened doors to further opportunities on the grand stage. His ability to immerse himself in a character and breathe life into the stories he portrayed became hallmarks of his performances, capturing the hearts of theatre-goers and critics alike.

His impressive Broadway credits continued to grow, with memorable roles in productions like "The Shadow Box" (1977), "The Iceman Cometh" (1985), and "The Grapes of Wrath" (1990). Each of these performances showcased his versatility and range, solidifying his reputation as an actor of exceptional talent and emotional depth.

For Mark Margolis, the early years in theatre were transformative not only in terms of his artistic growth but also in nurturing a profound love for the stage. The thrill of performing in front of live audiences and witnessing their reactions to his work became an integral part of his being as a storyteller.

His early theatre work taught him the nuances of stage presence, enabling him to command the attention of audiences and elicit genuine emotional responses. These experiences on the stage bolstered his confidence and reaffirmed his passion for the theatre, a love that remained an integral part of his life and career.

In conclusion, Mark Margolis's early career in theatre laid the foundation for a remarkable journey as an actor. The exposure to the Philadelphia theatre scene, formal training, collaboration with seasoned professionals, and his Broadway debut all contributed to shaping him into the versatile and respected actor he became. The early years in theatre not only honed his craft but also instilled in him a deep appreciation for the art of performance, leaving an enduring impact on his life's work as a masterful storyteller on the stage and screen.

His first film role

Mark Margolis's journey into the world of film commenced in the early 1970s, marking a significant expansion of his artistic repertoire beyond the realm of theatre. His first film role came in the 1972 crime-comedy "The Hot Rock," where he made a notable impression despite the limited screen time. This initial foray into the world of cinema opened doors for Margolis and set the stage for a series of pivotal film roles that would propel him further into the limelight.

In subsequent years, Mark Margolis continued to make his mark in the film industry with appearances in iconic productions. In 1974, he made a memorable contribution to "The Godfather Part II," the critically acclaimed sequel to Francis Ford Coppola's masterpiece. Although his role as Alberto Gutierrez, a Cuban rebel in the film, was relatively brief, it exemplified his ability to make a lasting impact in even the most minor parts.

Further showcasing his versatility as an actor, Margolis featured in the suspenseful thriller "The Taking of Pelham One Two Three" in 1974, sharing the screen with acting legends like Walter Matthau and Robert Shaw. His ability to hold his own alongside established stars marked him as a formidable talent with immense potential.

In 1976, Margolis's participation in the drama "The Last Tycoon," based on F. Scott Fitzgerald's unfinished novel, continued to solidify his presence in Hollywood. He held his own in scenes alongside acclaimed actors such as Robert De Niro and Jack Nicholson, earning praise for his contributions to the film.

As the 1980s dawned, Mark Margolis's trajectory in film continued to ascend, with more prominent roles coming his way. His memorable portrayal of Alberto ``The Shadow '' in the 1983 crime epic "Scarface" remains one of his most famous and enduring film roles. The ruthless Cuban drug dealer became an iconic character in the film, standing as a formidable adversary to Tony Montana, played by Al Pacino.

In the following years, Margolis's cinematic repertoire continued to grow, and his contributions to films like "The Cotton Club" (1984) and "The Mission" (1986) further showcased his adaptability as an actor. He effortlessly shifted between various genres, breathing life into a diverse range of characters and earning critical acclaim for his performances.

As the 1990s arrived, Margolis's cinematic journey continued with a string of captivating roles in films like "Requiem for a Dream" (2000) and "Analyse This" (1999). In addition to his film work, he ventured into television, captivating audiences as Alberto "The Shadow" again in "The Sopranos" (1999-2007).

Throughout his career in film, Mark Margolis's performances have been lauded by critics and celebrated by audiences. His versatility, coupled with his ability to bring depth and intensity to his characters, earned him accolades and recognition in the industry.

Mark Margolis's first film roles were not merely stepping stones but significant contributions to the world of cinema, solidifying his status as a respected and versatile actor. His ability to work seamlessly with celebrated actors and his unwavering commitment to his craft have made him an indispensable talent in the entertainment industry. Margolis's cinematic legacy is a testament to his immense talent and the profound impact he continues to make on audiences around the globe.

His work with Darren Aronofsky

Mark Margolis's collaboration with filmmaker Darren Aronofsky on three films is a testament to the strong working relationship they share, as well as Margolis's ability to bring depth and authenticity to even the smallest roles.

In *Pi*Mark Margolis's portrayal of Sol, the obsessed mathematician, showcases his exceptional ability to immerse himself in complex and enigmatic characters. Sol's relentless pursuit of a numerical code that holds the key to the universe is both captivating and unsettling, leaving a lasting impression on audiences.

In *Requiem for a Dream*Margolis takes on the role of Tyrone Coughlin, a drug dealer supplying heroin to Jared Leto's character, Harry Goldfarb. Tyrone's ruthless and violent nature is delivered with chilling authenticity by Margolis, leaving viewers with an unforgettable and haunting performance.

In *The Fountain*Mark Margolis's portrayal of Tom Creo, a determined scientist searching for a cure for his wife's cancer, demonstrates his ability to convey raw emotion and complexity in his characters. Tom's unwavering determination and resourcefulness evoke empathy from audiences and make Margolis's performance both moving and inspiring.

The collaboration between Mark Margolis and Darren Aronofsky has been lauded by critics and audiences alike. Aronofsky's distinct directorial style, coupled with Margolis's captivating performances, has resulted in a seamless fusion of storytelling and acting prowess, elevating the films to a higher level.

Beyond his work with Aronofsky, Margolis's talent has attracted collaborations with other esteemed filmmakers. Working alongside visionaries such as Martin Scorsese, Steven Spielberg, and Francis Ford Coppola, he has consistently delivered memorable performances that have enriched the films he graces with his presence.

Mark Margolis's body of work in film reflects his versatility and his dedication to his craft. Whether in a lead role or a supporting one, he brings a unique depth and intensity to his characters, leaving a lasting impact on audiences. His performances have garnered critical acclaim and awards recognition, solidifying his status as a respected and accomplished actor in the industry.

Mark Margolis's collaborations with Darren Aronofsky and other celebrated filmmakers stand as a testament to his commitment to his art and his remarkable ability to breathe life into every character he portrays. His contributions to the world of cinema have left an indelible mark, and his work continues to inspire and captivate audiences worldwide.

Chapter 3: Breaking Bad and Better Call Saul

Mark Margolis's portrayal of Hector Salamanca in *Breaking Bad* and *Better Call Saul* stands as a defining moment in his illustrious career. The character of Hector is a wheelchair-bound drug lord who communicates through the ringing of a bell, and Margolis's performance brought an unforgettable and multidimensional presence to the screen.

In *Breaking Bad*Hector Salamanca's entrance occurs in the second season of the series, and he is initially depicted as a frail and seemingly harmless elderly man. However, as the plot unfolds, the true extent of his power and danger becomes apparent. Hector's involvement in ordering the hit on Walter White's wife, Skyler, and his pivotal role in the demise of Gus Fring, a formidable rival drug lord, amplify the complexity of his character. Mark Margolis masterfully captures this dichotomy, infusing Hector with a chilling menace while also revealing moments of vulnerability and humanity.

Margolis's performance as Hector in *Breaking Bad* garnered widespread acclaim from critics and viewers alike. His portrayal of the menacing yet layered character played an integral role in elevating the series to the status of a television masterpiece. The Emmy Award nomination for Outstanding Guest Actor in a Drama Series in 2012 further solidified the recognition of his exceptional acting talent.

The success of *Breaking Bad* led to the prequel series, *Better Call Saul*, which delves deeper into the origins of characters, including Hector Salamanca. Margolis's reprisal of the role in *Better Call Saul* allowed him to expand on Hector's backstory, adding new dimensions to the character. Once again, Margolis's performance captivated audiences, revealing the nuances of Hector's early life and experiences that shaped the man he would become.

Mark Margolis's work on *Better Call Saul* not only complemented his performance in *Breaking Bad* but also stood as an independent testament to his exceptional acting ability. The actor's dedication to infusing each role with depth and authenticity shone through in his portrayal of Hector Salamanca, making him an essential and compelling presence in both series.

As a versatile and respected actor, Margolis's contributions to *Breaking Bad* and *Better Call Saul* cemented his place in television history. His ability to humanise and breathe life into complex characters has left an enduring impact on audiences. Mark Margolis's portrayal of Hector Salamanca will be remembered as one of the most captivating and memorable performances in the realm of television storytelling.

Margolis's role as Hector Salamanca

Mark Margolis's portrayal of Hector Salamanca in Breaking Bad is undeniably one of the most iconic and memorable characters in television history. Hector is a wheelchair-bound drug lord who communicates solely through ringing a bell, adding an element of intrigue and enigma to his persona. Margolis's exceptional performance as Hector elevates the character to new heights, making him a powerful and dangerous figure while also revealing his vulnerabilities and moments of humanity.

Introduced in the second season of Breaking Bad, Hector Salamanca is the uncle of Tuco Salamanca, a ruthless drug dealer whose fate is sealed by Walter White in the first season. Initially depicted as a frail and seemingly harmless old man, Hector's true persona is soon unveiled as a mastermind behind significant drug trade operations.

Throughout Breaking Bad, Hector's actions carry substantial consequences for the storyline. He orders a hit on Walter White's wife, Skyler, and plays a pivotal role in the demise of Gus Fring, the formidable rival drug lord. These actions showcase Hector's ruthless and cunning nature, making him an essential and unforgettable character within the series.

One of the most haunting and memorable moments featuring Hector Salamanca is when he rings his bell so forcefully that he suffers a heart attack. This scene encapsulates both his ruthlessness and vulnerability, leaving a lasting impact on viewers. Margolis's ability to portray such complexity with subtlety and authenticity is a testament to his mastery of his craft.

Mark Margolis's performance as Hector Salamanca goes beyond just chilling, as he brings a profound sense of sympathy and humanity to the character. This multi-layered portrayal allows viewers to empathise with Hector despite his villainous tendencies. His nuanced acting is one of the key elements that contributed to the immense success and critical acclaim of *Breaking Bad*.

In Better Call Saul, the prequel to *Breaking Bad*Margolis further enriches Hector's character through flashbacks to his early life. This expansion delves into his relationship with his brother and reveals the origins of his wheelchair, providing a deeper understanding of his transformation into the feared drug lord.

Mark Margolis's work on *Better Call Saul* once again showcases his exceptional talent as an actor, solidifying his place as one of the most respected figures in the industry. His portrayal of

Hector Salamanca remains a mesmerising and memorable contribution to television history, adding to his legacy as a versatile and gifted performer.

The impact of the role on his career

Mark Margolis's portrayal of Hector Salamanca indeed had a transformative effect on his career, catapulting him into the limelight and garnering him well-deserved recognition. The character's popularity and Margolis's exceptional performance led to prestigious award nominations and wins, which further solidified his reputation as a talented actor.

The Emmy Award nomination for Outstanding Guest Actor in a Drama Series in 2012 was a testament to Margolis's prowess in bringing Hector Salamanca to life. This prestigious nomination was a testament to the impact of his performance and the resonance the character had with both audiences and critics alike. Winning the 2013 Saturn Award for Best Guest Actor on Television added to Margolis's accolades, validating the remarkable depth and complexity he brought to the role.

The role of Hector Salamanca also opened up a plethora of new opportunities for Margolis in the entertainment industry. With increased visibility and recognition, he became an in-demand actor for various television and film projects. His appearances in other notable television shows like "American Horror Story: Asylum" and "Your Honor," as well as in acclaimed films like "Noah" and "The Irishman," showcased his versatility and further solidified his place in the industry.

Margolis's performance as Hector Salamanca left an indelible mark on television history. The character's complex nature and the nuanced portrayal by Margolis resonated deeply with audiences, making him an iconic figure in the realm of television villains. The role helped elevate Margolis's career to new heights and positioned him as an actor who could deliver exceptional performances in challenging and diverse roles.

In conclusion, the role of Hector Salamanca had a transformative impact on Mark Margolis's career, propelling him to greater prominence and recognition within the entertainment industry.

Margolis's exceptional portrayal of the character solidified his reputation as a talented actor, and his success in the role opened up new doors for him in his career, leading to diverse and engaging projects in television and film. Hector Salamanca remains one of the most memorable and iconic characters in television history, and Mark Margolis's portrayal will forever be celebrated as a masterful and unforgettable performance.

His Thoughts On The Show's Ending

Mark Margolis's satisfaction with the ending of *Breaking Bad* reflects the sentiment of many fans and critics who praised the series finale for its powerful and well-crafted conclusion. As an integral part of the show, Margolis's appreciation for the ending carries added significance, as it reflects the perspective of someone deeply involved in the series.

Margolis's belief that the ending was "true to the characters and to the story" highlights the importance of staying true to the character arcs and narrative established throughout the show. *Breaking Bad* was known for its meticulously developed characters, and their journeys were a central focus of the series. The ending managed to remain faithful to these arcs, providing a satisfying and authentic conclusion for both the main characters and supporting roles, including Hector Salamanca.

Margolis's admiration for the handling of Walter White's death underscores the emotional impact of the series finale. The death of the protagonist, played by Bryan Cranston, was a climactic and deeply affecting moment. Walter White's transformation from a mild-mannered high school chemistry teacher to a ruthless drug lord was central to the show's premise, and his ultimate fate carried significant weight. The scene was masterfully executed, capturing the full emotional weight of the consequences of Walter's actions and the impact they had on those around him.

The sense of closure Margolis mentioned as a vital aspect of the ending was crucial in providing a satisfying resolution for both the characters and the audience. After experiencing the characters' tumultuous journey over five intense seasons, viewers appreciated having their stories brought to a close in a meaningful and conclusive manner. The resolution offered a sense of redemption and closure for the characters, allowing the audience to reflect on their journeys and the consequences of their actions.

In conclusion, Mark Margolis's satisfaction with the ending of *Breaking Bad* highlights the show's success in delivering a fitting and authentic conclusion. The series finale managed to stay true to the characters and their arcs, while providing powerful and emotionally resonant moments that left a lasting impact on the audience. The ending provided a sense of closure, allowing the characters to find redemption and bringing the overall story to a satisfying close. As a respected actor who played a significant role in the series, Margolis's appreciation for the ending adds further validation to the widespread acclaim and admiration the show received.

Chapter 4: Other Notable Roles

Mark Margolis's career is indeed marked by a diverse range of memorable and impactful roles in film and television. Beyond his iconic portrayal of Hector Salamanca, he has delivered compelling performances in various projects that have showcased his versatility as an actor.

In "Scarface" (1983), Margolis portrayed Alberto "The Shadow," a ruthless Cuban drug dealer who encountered the film's protagonist, Tony Montana. Margolis's portrayal of this antagonist added depth to the film's complex narrative and contributed to the movie's status as a classic in the crime genre.

In "Requiem for a Dream" (2000), Margolis played the role of Tyrone Coughlin, a drug dealer who supplies heroin to the character Harry Goldfarb, played by Jared Leto. The film, known for its intense and harrowing depiction of addiction, showcased Margolis's ability to inhabit morally ambiguous characters with a gritty realism.

"The Fountain" (2006) provided another opportunity for Margolis to display his acting prowess. In this sci-fi drama, he portrayed Tom Creo, a scientist grappling with the search for a cure for his wife's cancer. The film delved into themes of love, mortality, and the pursuit of immortality, and Margolis's performance added emotional depth to the story.

"Constantine" (2005) saw Margolis take on the role of Felix Faust, a powerful demon intent on taking over the world. His portrayal of the menacing and supernatural character contributed to the film's dark and supernatural atmosphere.

More recently, in Martin Scorsese's "The Irishman" (2019), Margolis portrayed Sidney, a corrupt union official involved in organised crime. The film reunited Margolis with a celebrated director and showcased his ability to inhabit morally ambiguous characters with a captivating intensity.

Apart from these film roles, Margolis has left his mark on television with appearances in shows such as "The Sopranos," "Oz," "Law & Order," and "American Horror Story." His presence on the small screen has been equally impactful, and his performances have been praised by critics and audiences alike.

In conclusion, Mark Margolis's career is a testament to his talent and versatility as an actor. From his iconic portrayal of Hector Salamanca to his memorable roles in various films and television shows, he has consistently delivered intense and captivating performances. Margolis's contributions to the entertainment industry have earned him the respect and admiration of both his peers and audiences worldwide.

Margolis's work in Scarface, Oz, and Pi

Scarface (1983)

In "Scarface," Mark Margolis portrayed Alberto "The Shadow," a role that left a lasting impact on the film's narrative. As a ruthless Cuban drug dealer, The Shadow was a formidable adversary for Tony Montana, played by Al Pacino. Margolis's performance added depth to the character, and his portrayal of The Shadow's menacing and dangerous persona contributed to the film's intense and gripping atmosphere. The film's status as a crime classic is in part due to Margolis's compelling portrayal of this antagonist.

Oz (1997-2003)

In the HBO prison drama series "Oz," Margolis took on the role of Antonio Nappa, a powerful Italian mobster incarcerated for murder. His performance as Nappa was a masterclass in acting, blending elements of menace and vulnerability to create a multi-dimensional character. Margolis showcased Nappa's complex nature, portraying the character as both dangerous and human. The depth and authenticity he brought to the role earned him critical acclaim and a nomination for an Emmy Award for Outstanding Guest Actor in a Drama Series in 1998.

Pi (1998)

In Darren Aronofsky's psychological thriller "Pi," Margolis played Sol, a mathematician who becomes obsessed with finding the numerical code underlying the universe. Margolis's performance was enigmatic and captivating, capturing the intrigue and mystery of the film's plot. His portrayal of Sol's obsessive pursuit of knowledge and the ensuing psychological turmoil showcased Margolis's talent in immersing himself in complex characters. "Pi" was a visually stunning and thought-provoking film, and Margolis's contribution to the project was integral to its success.

These three roles exemplify Mark Margolis's ability to bring a wide range of characters to life. His performances in "Scarface," "Oz," and "Pi" have solidified his reputation as a versatile and skilled actor in the industry. Margolis's dedication to his craft and his ability to embody characters with intensity and authenticity have earned him the respect and admiration of critics and audiences alike. His work in these projects is a testament to his talent and commitment to his craft.

His other film and television roles

The Sopranos (1999-2007) as Angelo Garepe:

In "The Sopranos," Mark Margolis portrayed Angelo Garepe, a powerful New Jersey mobster and close associate of Tony Soprano, played by James Gandolfini. Margolis's performance as Garepe was a standout in the critically acclaimed series. He brought a sense of authenticity to the character, blending menace with vulnerability, making Garepe a complex and multi-dimensional figure. Margolis's ability to capture the nuances of Garepe's personality and his dynamic chemistry with the rest of the cast earned him praise from critics and audiences alike.

Requiem for a Dream (2000) as Tyrone Coughlin:

In "Requiem for a Dream," Margolis portrayed Tyrone Coughlin, a drug dealer who supplies heroin to Harry Goldfarb, played by Jared Leto. Margolis's portrayal of Tyrone was chilling and unforgettable, adding depth to this morally ambiguous character. He brought a sense of danger and despair to Tyrone, making him a compelling and sympathetic figure despite his criminal activities. Margolis's ability to convey the complexity of Tyrone's personality contributed to the emotional intensity of the film.

The Fountain (2006) as Tom Creo:

In Darren Aronofsky's visually stunning film "The Fountain," Margolis played Tom Creo, a scientist driven by the quest to find a cure for his wife's cancer. Margolis's performance as Tom was both moving and inspiring, bringing a sense of hope and determination to the character. His portrayal added emotional depth to the film, and he seamlessly conveyed the range of emotions that Tom experiences throughout the narrative. Margolis's collaboration with Aronofsky once again proved to be a successful pairing, contributing to the film's thought-provoking and visually captivating nature.

Constantine (2005) as Felix Faust:

In the supernatural action film "Constantine," Margolis portrayed Felix Faust, a powerful demon with sinister intentions. Margolis's performance as Faust was mesmerising, combining a menacing presence with charismatic allure. His portrayal of the character added to the film's dark and mystical atmosphere, making Faust a formidable adversary to the protagonist, John Constantine, portrayed by Keanu Reeves. Margolis's ability to embody this enigmatic and malevolent character was a testament to his skill as an actor.

The Irishman (2019) as Sidney Berkowitz:

In Martin Scorsese's crime epic "The Irishman," Margolis played Sidney Berkowitz, a corrupt union official involved in organised crime. Margolis's portrayal of Sidney was chilling and believable, contributing to the film's authenticity and gripping narrative. He brought a sense of menace and danger to the role, making Sidney a character that left a lasting impression on audiences. Margolis's collaboration with Scorsese was yet another example of his ability to seamlessly integrate into diverse and complex projects.

Mark Margolis's career is filled with a multitude of notable roles across film and television. His versatility as an actor, combined with his ability to delve into the intricacies of various characters, has earned him praise and respect in the industry. His performances in "The Sopranos," "Requiem for a Dream," "The Fountain," "Constantine," and "The Irishman" are a testament to his talent and dedication to his craft. Margolis's contribution to these projects has left a lasting impact on audiences and solidified his position as a respected actor in the entertainment world.

Chapter 5: Personal Life

Early Life and Education:

Mark Margolis was born on November 26, 1939, in Philadelphia, Pennsylvania, to Isidore Margolis and Fanya Fried. His father worked in a factory, while his mother was a homemaker. He grew up with one brother, Jerome, in a household that encouraged creativity and expression. Margolis's passion for the arts began at a young age, and he was drawn to theatre and dance.

Margolis's interest in acting led him to attend the Philadelphia High School for the Creative and Performing Arts. There, he honed his skills in theatre and dance, laying the foundation for his future career as an actor. After graduating, he pursued further training at the prestigious Actors Studio in New York City, where he refined his craft and gained invaluable insights into the world of acting.

Advocacy for the Arts and Charity Work:

While Mark Margolis may prefer to keep his personal life private, his dedication to the arts and charitable endeavours has been more visible. He has been a passionate advocate for the importance of arts education and the support of the creative community.

Margolis has been actively involved in several charitable organisations, using his platform and influence to contribute to causes he cares about deeply. His commitment to supporting the arts and charitable causes has made him a respected figure in both the entertainment industry and the philanthropic community.

Legacy:

Throughout his illustrious career, Mark Margolis has proven himself to be a versatile and talented actor. His ability to portray a wide range of characters with intensity and depth has earned him critical acclaim and the admiration of audiences worldwide. From powerful mobsters to enigmatic drug dealers and complex scientists, Margolis's performances have left an indelible mark on the films and television shows in which he appeared.

Despite his success and acclaim, Margolis has remained true to his private nature, focusing on his craft and family life. He continues to be an influential figure in the entertainment industry, admired for his dedication to the art of acting and his commitment to using his platform for positive impact. As a beloved and respected actor, Mark Margolis's legacy in the world of film and television will undoubtedly endure for generations to come.

Margolis's marriage and children

Mark Margolis has had two marriages in his life. His first marriage was to Jacqueline Petcove, and the couple remained together for an impressive 61 years until Jacqueline's passing in 2023. Throughout their long marriage, they shared a life filled with love and support for each other. The details of their relationship have been kept private, and they successfully maintained a low profile when it came to their personal life.

From their union, Mark and Jacqueline had one son, Morgan H. Margolis. Morgan followed in his father's footsteps, pursuing a career in the entertainment industry. He became a successful producer and CEO of Knitting Factory Entertainment, a prominent music and media company. Morgan's involvement in the entertainment business further deepened the Margolis family's connection to the creative arts.

After the passing of his first wife, Mark Margolis married Barbara Margolis in 2009. Their marriage, however, came to an end, and they divorced in 2012. Mark's private nature has led him to keep the details of his personal life away from the public eye, and he rarely discusses his relationships or family matters.

Family Values and Advocacy for the Arts:

Although Mark Margolis is known for his intense and memorable on-screen performances, he has consistently emphasised the importance of family in his life. He has acknowledged that his family is his top priority, showing a deep appreciation for the love and support they provide.

Beyond his work as an actor, Margolis has also demonstrated a strong commitment to the arts. He is a passionate advocate for arts education and the support of creative endeavours. As a member of the board of directors for both the Actors Studio and the New York Public Theater, he actively contributes to nurturing talent and preserving the cultural significance of the performing arts.

Conclusion:

Mark Margolis is not only a remarkable actor with a diverse and successful career, but he also values the importance of family and has demonstrated his dedication to supporting the arts. His private nature has allowed him to protect the personal aspects of his life, but his achievements and influence in the entertainment industry are undeniably significant. Margolis's legacy as an actor and his commitment to the arts will continue to inspire and resonate with both audiences and aspiring artists for years to come.

His hobbies and interests

Mark Margolis's hobbies and interests add depth to his persona as a versatile and talented actor. Here's a closer look at how these passions contribute to his well-rounded nature:

Reading: Margolis's love for reading provides him with an escape from the demands of his profession. Engaging with different literary works allows him to immerse himself in new worlds and gain insights into various cultures, which can enrich his understanding of the human experience. It also offers him a way to continuously learn and expand his horizons beyond acting.

Music: The diverse range of music genres that Margolis enjoys listening to reflects his appreciation for the emotional power of music. Just like acting, music can evoke emotions, and he likely draws inspiration from different musical styles that resonate with his varied roles. Additionally, music can serve as a creative outlet and a source of relaxation in his busy life.

Art: Margolis's interest in art aligns with his involvement in the performing arts. He likely finds inspiration from various artistic expressions, using them to enrich his performances and deepen his understanding of human behaviour. Visiting museums and galleries may provide him with a unique perspective on storytelling and the visual representation of emotions.

Travel: As a traveller, Margolis embraces opportunities to experience different cultures, which can influence his portrayal of characters from diverse backgrounds. Exposure to different ways of life and cultural practices can inform his acting choices, enhancing the authenticity of his performances.

Nature: The outdoors provide Margolis with a retreat from the hustle and bustle of the entertainment industry. Engaging in activities like hiking, camping, and fishing allows him to find solace in nature, fostering a sense of inner peace and rejuvenation. This connection to nature can also inspire his performances, as he taps into the tranquillity and beauty of the natural world.

Mark Margolis's hobbies and interests offer a glimpse into his multi-faceted personality. Beyond being a talented actor, he demonstrates a genuine curiosity for life, constantly seeking new experiences and sources of inspiration. His well-roundedness contributes to his ability to bring depth and complexity to the characters he portrays, making him an even more remarkable and respected figure in the entertainment industry.

His Thoughts On Retirement

Mark Margolis's thoughts on retirement reflect a thoughtful and introspective approach to his career and personal life:

Not Sure About Retirement: Margolis's uncertainty about retirement is understandable given his passion for acting and the fulfilment he derives from his work. As an actor, he continues to challenge himself with diverse roles and brings depth to his performances, indicating that he still finds joy in the craft. This uncertainty also shows his willingness to be flexible and adapt to changing circumstances.

Spending Time with Family: Margolis's desire to spend more time with his family is a testament to his values and priorities. Despite his busy schedule as an actor, he recognizes the importance of nurturing his personal relationships and creating lasting memories with his loved ones. Retirement would provide him the opportunity to focus on family bonding and create a stronger support system.

Continuing Involvement in the Arts: Margolis's vision for his post-retirement life highlights his enduring commitment to the world of arts. His interest in teaching acting and directing plays showcases a desire to pass on his wealth of knowledge and experience to the next generation of performers. Additionally, his interest in writing and producing films signifies a desire to explore new creative avenues and contribute to the industry from a different perspective.

Mark Margolis's contemplation of retirement demonstrates his thoughtful and deliberate approach to both his career and personal life. He is willing to embrace new possibilities while staying true to his values and passions. Whether he continues acting or embarks on new ventures, it is evident that he will bring the same dedication and commitment to any endeavour he pursues.

His multifaceted approach to life and the arts will undoubtedly leave a lasting impact on the entertainment industry and those he interacts with, both professionally and personally.

Chapter 6: Legacy

Margolis's impact on the entertainment industry

Mark Margolis's legacy in the entertainment industry extends beyond his remarkable performances. He has left an indelible mark through his versatility, intense portrayals, and ability to bring complex characters to life. His work has not only entertained but also inspired others in the industry, leaving a lasting impact that will be remembered for years to come.

Inspiring Aspiring Actors: Margolis's dedication to his craft and his ability to tackle challenging roles have served as an inspiration to aspiring actors. His journey from studying theatre and dance to becoming a respected actor in film and television is a testament to hard work and perseverance. Many young actors look up to him as a role model, striving to emulate his success and dedication to the art form.

Creating Memorable Characters: Margolis's performances have brought some of the most memorable characters to the screen. From the menacing Hector Salamanca in *Breaking Bad* to the enigmatic Sol in *Pi*His portrayals have resonated with audiences worldwide. These characters have become iconic and have left a lasting impression on the cultural landscape of the entertainment industry.

Challenging and Believable Characters: Margolis's ability to delve into the complexities of his characters and make them believable has garnered him critical acclaim. His performances transcend the screen, evoking genuine emotions from audiences and immersing them in the story. This authenticity has set a high standard for character portrayal in film and television.

A Lasting Legacy: As time goes on, Margolis's impact will continue to inspire and influence generations of actors and creators. His contributions to the industry will be celebrated as part of the rich tapestry of cinematic history. Through his work, he has left an enduring legacy that will be cherished by fans and professionals alike.

In conclusion, Mark Margolis's legacy is a testament to his talent, versatility, and dedication to his craft. He has created unforgettable characters, inspired aspiring actors, and set a high standard for performances in the entertainment industry. His work will continue to captivate audiences and influence future generations, making him a cherished and respected figure in the world of film and television.

His fans and admirers

Mark Margolis's fans and admirers span a wide and diverse audience, drawn together by their admiration for his exceptional talent and captivating performances. From his role as Hector Salamanca in *Breaking Bad* to his appearances in other films and television shows, Margolis has garnered a devoted following that continues to grow.

1. Fans of Breaking Bad: Margolis's portrayal of Hector Salamanca in *Breaking Bad* and its prequel *Better Call Saul* has earned him a dedicated and passionate fan base. His

performance as the wheelchair-bound drug lord, communicating through the ringing of a bell, left a profound impact on viewers. Fans of the show appreciate his ability to convey emotions and depth to a character with limited verbal communication, making Hector Salamanca one of the most memorable and iconic characters in television history.

2. Fans of Other Films and Television Shows:

In addition to Breaking Bad, Margolis's work in other films and television shows has also garnered him admirers. Fans of Scarface appreciate his portrayal of Alberto "The Shadow," a ruthless Cuban drug dealer whose demise at the hands of Tony Montana is etched into cinema history. Likewise, fans of *Requiem for a Dream admires Margolis's portrayal of

Tyrone Coughlin, a drug dealer whose chilling presence adds to the intensity of the film.

3. Actors and Directors: Margolis's talent has earned him admiration from fellow actors and directors in the industry. Vince Gilligan, the creator of Breaking Bad has spoken highly of Margolis, calling him one of his favourite actors. Darren Aronofsky, the director of Requiem for a Dream, has praised Margolis as one of the most talented actors he has ever worked with. Such accolades from esteemed industry figures speak to the respect and recognition Margolis has earned among his peers.

Mark Margolis's fans and admirers come from all walks of life, unified by their appreciation for his craft and the indelible impact he has made on the entertainment industry. His ability to bring complex and nuanced characters to life, coupled with his versatile acting skills, has solidified his position as a respected and cherished figure in the world of film and television. As his career continues to evolve, Margolis's legacy as an exceptional actor and captivating performer will undoubtedly endure, captivating audiences and inspiring future generations of talent.

His lasting legacy

Mark Margolis's lasting legacy is one that will undoubtedly endure and leave a profound impact on the entertainment industry. His contributions as a versatile and talented actor have solidified his position as a revered figure among audiences and his peers. Here are some key aspects of

Mark Margolis's lasting legacy:

1. Enduring Enjoyment by Audiences: Margolis's work, particularly his performances as Hector Salamanca in *Breaking Bad* and *Better Call Saul*, will continue to be cherished and admired by audiences for generations. These iconic portrayals have become ingrained in popular culture, ensuring that Margolis's legacy will remain alive through the enjoyment of his performances for years to come.

2. Inspiring Aspiring Actors: Margolis's talent and dedication to his craft will serve as an inspiration for aspiring actors. He demonstrated the power of bringing complex and challenging characters to life, proving that with dedication and skill, actors can leave a lasting impact on the

industry. His work will motivate future generations to pursue their dreams and tackle roles that push the boundaries of their abilities.

3. Reverence from Industry Professionals: Margolis's work has earned him admiration and reverence from fellow actors, directors, and industry professionals. His ability to immerse himself in his characters and deliver intense performances has garnered respect from those within the entertainment world. His legacy will continue to be celebrated and appreciated by his colleagues, further solidifying his position as a highly respected actor.

4. Continued Study of His Performances: Margolis's performances will continue to be studied by actors and directors as examples of exceptional acting. His ability to bring complex characters to life in a nuanced and captivating manner will serve as a reference point for those seeking to enhance their own skills in the craft of acting.

Mark Margolis's legacy extends beyond the screen, reaching the hearts of audiences and inspiring future generations of actors. His contributions have left an indelible mark on the entertainment industry, solidifying his place as a talented and versatile actor. As his work continues to be enjoyed and admired, Margolis's legacy as a respected and cherished figure in the world of film and television will endure for years to come.

Interesting and fun facts

1. Early Artistic Education: Mark Margolis's passion for the arts began at an early age. He attended the Philadelphia High School for the Creative and Performing Arts, where he honed his skills in theatre and dance, setting the foundation for his successful acting career.

2. Actor Studio Training: Margolis further sharpened his acting abilities by studying at the prestigious Actors Studio in New York City. This renowned institution has produced some of the finest actors in the industry, and Margolis's training there undoubtedly contributed to his remarkable performances.

3. Memorable Scarface Role: One of Margolis's breakthrough roles was in Brian De Palma's crime epic Scarface (1983), where he portrayed the chilling character of Alberto "The Shadow," a ruthless Cuban drug dealer. This memorable performance garnered attention and set the stage for his future success.

4. Versatility in Acting: Throughout his career, Margolis has demonstrated his versatility as an actor. He can seamlessly transition from playing menacing villains to complex and sympathetic characters, showcasing his ability to tackle a diverse range of roles.

5. Emmy Award Nomination: Margolis received critical acclaim for his portrayal of Hector Salamanca in *Breaking Bad* and *Better Call Saul*, earning him a nomination for an Emmy Award for Outstanding Guest Actor in a Drama Series. This recognition highlights the depth and brilliance of his performances.

6. Talented Musician: Apart from acting, Margolis is a skilled guitarist and singer. He has been part of various musical bands and has enjoyed sharing his musical talents with others.

7. Passion for Literature: As an avid reader, Margolis finds solace in literature. He enjoys delving into various genres, including fiction, nonfiction, and poetry. His passion for reading adds to his artistic and intellectual repertoire.

8. Jazz Enthusiast: Margolis's love for jazz music is evident in his music preferences. He enjoys the works of jazz legends like Miles Davis, John Coltrane, and Thelonious Monk, appreciating the genre's expressive and emotive qualities.

9. Charitable Involvement: Margolis's passion for the arts extends to his charitable endeavours. He actively supports organisations like the Actors Studio, the New York Public Theater, and the American Theatre Wing, demonstrating his commitment to promoting and preserving the arts.

10. Family-Oriented: Despite his success, Margolis remains a private person who prioritises his family above all else. He cherishes his time with loved ones and values the bond they share.

Mark Margolis's multifaceted interests and talents make him an intriguing and accomplished individual both on and off-screen. His contributions to the entertainment industry, coupled with his involvement in charitable causes, showcase his passion for the arts and commitment to making a positive impact in the world. As his legacy continues to resonate with audiences, Mark Margolis's influence on the entertainment industry will be remembered and celebrated for years to come.

Printed in Great Britain
by Amazon

28323368R00056